Select fables from Gulistan, or the bed of roses. Translated from the original Persian of Sadi, by Stephen Sulivan, Esq.

Saâdi

Eighteenth Century
Collections Online
Print Editions

Gale ECCO Print Editions

Relive history with *Eighteenth Century Collections Online*, now available in print for the independent historian and collector. This series includes the most significant English-language and foreign-language works printed in Great Britain during the eighteenth century, and is organized in seven different subject areas including literature and language; medicine, science, and technology; and religion and philosophy. The collection also includes thousands of important works from the Americas.

The eighteenth century has been called "The Age of Enlightenment." It was a period of rapid advance in print culture and publishing, in world exploration, and in the rapid growth of science and technology – all of which had a profound impact on the political and cultural landscape. At the end of the century the American Revolution, French Revolution and Industrial Revolution, perhaps three of the most significant events in modern history, set in motion developments that eventually dominated world political, economic, and social life.

In a groundbreaking effort, Gale initiated a revolution of its own: digitization of epic proportions to preserve these invaluable works in the largest online archive of its kind. Contributions from major world libraries constitute over 175,000 original printed works. Scanned images of the actual pages, rather than transcriptions, recreate the works ***as they first appeared.***

Now for the first time, these high-quality digital scans of original works are available via print-on-demand, making them readily accessible to libraries, students, independent scholars, and readers of all ages.

For our initial release we have created seven robust collections to form one the world's most comprehensive catalogs of 18th century works.

Initial Gale ECCO Print Editions collections include:

> ***History and Geography***
> Rich in titles on English life and social history, this collection spans the world as it was known to eighteenth-century historians and explorers. Titles include a wealth of travel accounts and diaries, histories of nations from throughout the world, and maps and charts of a world that was still being discovered. Students of the War of American Independence will find fascinating accounts from the British side of conflict.

Social Science
Delve into what it was like to live during the eighteenth century by reading the first-hand accounts of everyday people, including city dwellers and farmers, businessmen and bankers, artisans and merchants, artists and their patrons, politicians and their constituents. Original texts make the American, French, and Industrial revolutions vividly contemporary.

Medicine, Science and Technology
Medical theory and practice of the 1700s developed rapidly, as is evidenced by the extensive collection, which includes descriptions of diseases, their conditions, and treatments. Books on science and technology, agriculture, military technology, natural philosophy, even cookbooks, are all contained here.

Literature and Language
Western literary study flows out of eighteenth-century works by Alexander Pope, Daniel Defoe, Henry Fielding, Frances Burney, Denis Diderot, Johann Gottfried Herder, Johann Wolfgang von Goethe, and others. Experience the birth of the modern novel, or compare the development of language using dictionaries and grammar discourses.

Religion and Philosophy
The Age of Enlightenment profoundly enriched religious and philosophical understanding and continues to influence present-day thinking. Works collected here include masterpieces by David Hume, Immanuel Kant, and Jean-Jacques Rousseau, as well as religious sermons and moral debates on the issues of the day, such as the slave trade. The Age of Reason saw conflict between Protestantism and Catholicism transformed into one between faith and logic -- a debate that continues in the twenty-first century.

Law and Reference
This collection reveals the history of English common law and Empire law in a vastly changing world of British expansion. Dominating the legal field is the *Commentaries of the Law of England* by Sir William Blackstone, which first appeared in 1765. Reference works such as almanacs and catalogues continue to educate us by revealing the day-to-day workings of society.

Fine Arts
The eighteenth-century fascination with Greek and Roman antiquity followed the systematic excavation of the ruins at Pompeii and Herculaneum in southern Italy; and after 1750 a neoclassical style dominated all artistic fields. The titles here trace developments in mostly English-language works on painting, sculpture, architecture, music, theater, and other disciplines. Instructional works on musical instruments, catalogs of art objects, comic operas, and more are also included.

The BiblioLife Network

This project was made possible in part by the BiblioLife Network (BLN), a project aimed at addressing some of the huge challenges facing book preservationists around the world. The BLN includes libraries, library networks, archives, subject matter experts, online communities and library service providers. We believe every book ever published should be available as a high-quality print reproduction; printed on-demand anywhere in the world. This insures the ongoing accessibility of the content and helps generate sustainable revenue for the libraries and organizations that work to preserve these important materials.

The following book is in the "public domain" and represents an authentic reproduction of the text as printed by the original publisher. While we have attempted to accurately maintain the integrity of the original work, there are sometimes problems with the original work or the micro-film from which the books were digitized. This can result in minor errors in reproduction. Possible imperfections include missing and blurred pages, poor pictures, markings and other reproduction issues beyond our control. Because this work is culturally important, we have made it available as part of our commitment to protecting, preserving, and promoting the world's literature.

GUIDE TO FOLD-OUTS MAPS and OVERSIZED IMAGES

The book you are reading was digitized from microfilm captured over the past thirty to forty years. Years after the creation of the original microfilm, the book was converted to digital files and made available in an online database.

In an online database, page images do not need to conform to the size restrictions found in a printed book. When converting these images back into a printed bound book, the page sizes are standardized in ways that maintain the detail of the original. For large images, such as fold-out maps, the original page image is split into two or more pages

Guidelines used to determine how to split the page image follows:

- Some images are split vertically; large images require vertical and horizontal splits.
- For horizontal splits, the content is split left to right.
- For vertical splits, the content is split from top to bottom.
- For both vertical and horizontal splits, the image is processed from top left to bottom right.

SELECT FABLES

FROM

GULISTAN,

OR THE

BED OF ROSES.

TRANSLATED FROM THE

ORIGINAL PERSIAN OF SADÍ,

BY

STEPHEN SULIVAN, Esq.

LONDON:
Printed for J. RIDLEY, in St. James's Street.
MDCCLXXIV.

THE PREFACE.

IT is a received notion, that the Persian language is little else than a jumble of bombast and extravagance; that it is full of absurd phrases and incoherent allusions; and if any thing like sense is discoverable, that it is so thinly scattered, as to escape an ordinary discernment. That this is a vulgar error, and that the observation does not hold true in all cases, the fables of Sadi afford a striking example. The stile (as far as I am capable judging) appears to me to be pure, simple, and elegant: the allusions

allusions are beautiful, and, though often accompanied with that wildness which is the peculiar characteristic of Oriental Genius, it is seldom, if ever, difficult to ascertain their precise meaning. As the Gulistan, or Bed of Roses, from whence this small specimen is selected, is mentioned in very high terms, by a Gentleman of acknowledged abilities and universal talents, in his Introduction to the Persian Grammar, it excited my curiosity: and all that it becomes me to add, is, that my best endeavours have been exerted to convey a tolerable idea of the original.

I cannot omit in this place my particular obligations to Mr. SAVAGE, who resided in Persia many years, as principal Manager for the East-India Company, with equal credit to himself,

self, and benefit to his Employers; and whose abilities and experience as a Director require no panegyric from me. It is to this Gentleman's politeness and friendship that I am indebted for several manuscripts of the Persian language, without which I could not have attained even to that moderate progress which I have hitherto made. I have only to lament, that Sadi has not the good fortune of Cicero. Sadi is introduced to the English reader under every possible disadvantage; whilst every spark of Cicero's fire remains, as often as Mr. MELMOTH transfuses the spirit of that greatest of all writers into his own masterly compositions.

Stephen Sulivan.

FABLES.

FABLE I.

A Gang of thieves of Arabia were sitting upon the top of a mountain, and stopped the passage of the caravan. The inhabitants of the cities were wearied out by their stratagems, and the Sultan's army defeated; for they had secured a fortified place upon the top of the mountain, and fixed upon it as their own dwelling and habitation.

The Heads of Assembly advised together what methods they should take to prevent their plunder; because, if this gang should gain an establishment in this manner on the top of the mountain, all possibility of coping with them must be at an end.

A tree that has but just taken root may be removed by the strength of a single person; if you let it alone, it will grow so high, that you cannot then root it up from its foundation. At first you may stop the head of a spring with a bit of cork; but when it has kept running for some time, and filled the country, an elephant is not able to pass it.

Word was immediately given to send out a party to be spies on the motions of the gang, and to watch the time when, at a convenient opportunity, they were going to attack another caravan, and their habitation was left empty. They then dispatched some of their most experienced people, who had been tried in battle, who hid themselves in the valley of the mountain. At night the thieves returned home, having travelled far and found booty. They laid down their arms, and deposited their spoils. The first enemy that attacked them was

was sleep, and they slept till a quarter of the night was spent The circle of the sun was now gone down in darkness; then it was Jonas was swallowed up by the whale. The men jumped out of their ambuscade, and tied the hands of every one of them behind. The next morning they brought them all to the palace before the King, who issued his orders that every one of them should be put to death.

In the number of this gang there was a young man, who had just arrived at the opening blossom of youth, and the down had but newly spread itself over the flower of his cheek. One of the Viceroys kissed the feet of the King's throne, and with a face of supplication bent himself to the earth, and said, " This lad to this moment
" has gathered no fruit from the garden
" of his youth, and hath as yet derived no
" enjoyment from the plant of his life.
" My hopes are placed therefore in the
" kindness and generosity of my master,
" who, by sparing his blood, may bestow
" an obligation upon his servant."

The King turned away at these words, because they were not agreeable to him, and said, "Whosoever is bad in principle, "can never take example from the good: "education to a bad principle is like a ball "placed at the top of a dome. It is better "to destroy the wicked generation of all "such people, and to root up the founda- "tion of their families; for to extinguish "a fire and leave a spark, and to kill a "viper and preserve its young ones, is "not acting like wise men. Though the "cloud should pour down the water of "life, you can gather no fruit from the "bough of the willow. Do not waste "your time with the worthless: no sugar "can you get from the bamboo."

The Viceroy approved of this saying, was more and more pleased with it, applauded the King for the justice of the thought, and said, "May it please your "Majesty, what the King has now uttered "is the very truth, and it is an excuse that "is unanswerable; but still your servant "has hopes, that in the company of the
"virtuous

" virtuous he may receive the education
" of virtue, and acquire the difpofition of
" good men; for he is but a child, and
" that temper of rebellion and enmity, fo
" plain in the reft of the gang, does not
" feem as yet to have fettled in his nature.
" The fon of Noah kept company with
" bad men; by this means he loft the re-
" putation of his father's prophecy. The
" dog of the difciples of Kyf, * by fol-
" lowing their fteps for fome time, became
" good, and was held facred."

Thus faid the Viceroy, and a multitude of courtiers joined with him in fupplicating

* The difciples of Kyf were an order of religious men; and whenever they fet out upon a pilgrimage, they were conftantly accompanied by this dog. The ftory goes, that in the way it was neceffary for them to take, there was a dragon; and when they came near to the place, the dog began barking fo violently, that they were alarmed, and turned back; otherwife they muft have fallen into the jaws of the dragon. This explanation of the " dog of the difciples of Kyf " was communicated to me by a native of Perfia, who fays, that the traditional fuperftition concerning this dog holds to this day.

ting the King for the young man's pardon, till the King at last desisted from his resolution, and said, " I pardon him, though I
" see no reason: you know what King
" Zal said formerly to the hero Rustum—
" An enemy ought never to be reckoned
" weak or contemptible. Many a time
" have we seen the water at the head of a
" small spring, how, when it has aug-
" mented its course, it has been able to
" carry away with it a camel and his load."

In short, they brought up the young man with a great deal of indulgence and expence; and appointed a proper instructor to take care of his education, 'till such time as he had been taught how to prefer a request with politeness, and to refuse a suit with a good grace, and was made acquainted with all the ceremonies at court; and indeed, as far as this went, he was pleasing to every body.

One day the Viceroy was speaking of his temper in the King's presence, that the good education he had received had worked

an

an effect in him, and that he was now polished out of his former rusticity. The King laughed, and said, " A young wolf, " let him be caressed ever so much, will " turn out a wolf at last: a person once was " bringing up a young wolf, and when he " was bred up, he tore his master in " pieces." A year after this, a set of vagabonds of the city entered into a conspiracy with this young man; and when they found a convenient opportunity, they killed the Viceroy, with both his sons, and carried off an immense quantity of riches, and retreated as criminals, for safety, to the cave at the foot of the mountain, where they succeeded the former gang of their ancestors.

The next morning they communicated to the King all that had happened. The King bit the finger of Amazement with the teeth of Sorrow, and said, " How can " a man make a good sword out of bad " iron? he who is good for nothing, will " never rise to be a person of real con- " sequence. There is no difference in the

" fruitful

"fruitful quality of the rain; but a tulip
"grows in the garden, and straw in bad
"ground: bad ground will never produce
"a hyacinth. Waste not the seed of
"hope in it. To do good to bad peo-
"ple, is exactly the same as to do ill, in-
"stead of well, to good people."

FABLE II.

I was sitting in a boat with a multitude of wise people. A small vessel sunk behind us, and two brothers were carried down. One of the wise men said to a sailor, "Take them both up, and I will "give you a thousand dynars." Whilst the sailor was taking up one of them, the other died. I said to him, "That poor "fellow is dead already: for this reason "you delayed to catch hold of him, and "made such haste with the other." The sailor laughed, and replied, "What you "say is certainly true: but otherwise it "was more my intention to save this man, "because once I was left alone in a de- "sert, this man set me upon a camel, and "from the other, in my infancy, I received "a whipping."

I said,

I said, " All merciful God! he who did good, has been rewarded with good for himself; and he who did bad, has been punished with evil. As long as you can, hurt nobody; for in the road there may be thorns: advance the affairs of the poor distressed man, because you also may have affairs of your own."

FABLE

FABLE III.

A Dervise was one of the King's guests. When he sat down to dinner, he ate less than was his inclination; and when he rose up to prayer, he prayed more than was his usual custom, that an opinion of his goodness might be increased. O Arabian! I fear thou wilt not reach Mecca; for the road which you are now taking, leads you to Turkey.

When he returned home, he desired a table might be set out for dinner. The Dervise had a very sensible son, who said, "O father, perhaps you ate nothing in the "King's company?" He replied, "I ate "nothing, that my not eating might "carry an appearance of mortification, "and be of service to me with the King." The son answered, "Give over praying
' then;

" then; for you have not one prayer left
" that can be of use to you."

O thou, that with the open palm of the hand makest an ostentatious display of thy good qualities, and concealest under the arm thy bad qualities, what canst thou expect to buy, O proud man, in the day of misfortune, with thy false coin?

FABLE

FABLE IV.

THEY were praising one of the holy men in a company, and were enumerating his amiable qualities: he raised up his head, and said, "I know my-"self: my character appears good in the "eyes of the world; but my head is "bowed down with shame from the bad-"ness of my heart. The world praises the "peacock for his spots, and beautiful co-"lour; and he takes shame to himself "from his ugly feet."

FABLE V.

THERE was a person who had arrived at a superior knowledge in boxing: his master had taught him three hundred and fifty-nine ways of fighting; but there was one manner of fighting which he had not yet taught him, and he delayed continually in making him acquainted with this manner. The scholar however was superior to the master in strength and appearance; and nobody, in short, was able to cope with him.

One day he said to the King, "The su-
"periority which my master has over me,
"is from his situation, and from the credit
"which the world gives him: and if it
"does not lie here, I maintain, I am not
"inferior to him in strength; and in the
"knowledge of boxing, his equal."

This saying appeared strange to the King: he gave orders to fix upon a large piece of ground; and they brought together all the strong people; and the courtiers and attendants of the King were present.

The boy came in like a drunken elephant, and with such pride, that, if there had been a mountain of iron, he would have taken it from its place. The master perceived he could not beat his scholar: he closed in with him, therefore, by the help of that curious manner which he had concealed from him, took him up, held him over his head, and dashed him upon the ground.

The multitude shouted; the King gave orders to bestow upon the master fine garments and riches, and reprimanded the boy, that he should make himself equal to him who had instructed him, when he could not stand in competition with him.

[16]

The boy said, "O King, in the know-
"ledge of boxing he concealed from me
"one manner of fighting; by that very
"manner he conquered me." The master
replied, "I reserved it for myself for such
"a day as this. Either gratitude never
"was in the world, or no one has prac-
"tised it: no one ever learnt the art of
"shooting from me, who did not hit me
"at last."

FABLE

FABLE VI.

I Remember, that in the time of my infancy I was very religious: I watched all night, and was punctual at prayers.

One night I was sitting in the presence of my father, and for the whole night I never closed my eyes, and I kept the Alcoran in my bosom. A number of people were sleeping round us. I said to my father, 'None of these people rise up to 'perform their worship; they are so bu-'ried in the sleep of forgetfulness, that 'you would think they were dead.'

The father replied, 'O son, if you 'you would sleep also, it would be better 'for you, because you would then be like 'the rest of your fellow creatures. The 'boaster sees no other person good but 'himself, because he draws the curtain of
'pride

'pride before his eye: if he could find
'an eye to see God, he would see no one
'worse than himself.'

FABLE VII.

SOME robbers had plundered a caravan in Greece, and had taken a great quantity of riches. The merchants made terrible mourning and lamentation, and beseeched them, in the name of their Prophet, to restore what they had taken. All was to no purpose.

There was a celebrated Doctor in the caravan, whose name was Lockman. One of the passengers said to him, 'Utter some
'wise sentence or other to these people,
'that you recollect from your studies.
'perhaps they will leave us our money;
'it will be a great mortification to have
'such a quantity of riches thrown away.'

The Doctor replied, 'To give any ad-
'vice to such wretches, is a mortification
'indeed: from the iron that the rust hath
'eaten away, it is impossible, by rubbing,
'to rub out the spots. To what purpose
'is it to deliver instruction to a wicked
'heart? A nail will not enter into a
'stone. Be attentive and labour for the
'prosperity of the poor man; for the
'peace of the poor man's mind will keep
'misfortune far from thee. When the
'beggar with humility petitions thy alms,
'give him, or the oppressor shall employ
'force against thee.'

FABLE VIII.

I Saw a religious man upon the bank of a river: he had received a wound from a leopard, and there was no medicine that could heal it: he was in pain for a long time, but was constantly offering up his thanksgiving to God, who is powerful and good. They asked him, 'What are you giving thanks for?' He replied, 'Because I suffer from misfortune, not from guilt: and, if that God, the friend whom I love, was to give me up to be killed without mercy, that you may not imagine, that in that hour my life would be my concern, I should say, "What crime has your poor servant committed, that has caused your displeasure against him?" *That* would be my concern.'

FABLE IX.

ONE of the slaves of Omer Lys ran away. The people went after him, and brought him back. The Viceroy had a resentment against him, and issued his orders to kill him, that the other slaves might not commit the like offence. The slave bent his head to the ground in the presence of Omer, and said, 'What-
'ever may happen to me, since it is
'thy pleasure, is right. What demand
'can a slave make, when the power be-
'longs to his master? But because I have
'been educated at the expence of this
'family, I do not wish that thou should'st
'be punished at the day of judgement for
'shedding my blood. If thou hast a
'desire to kill me, do it according to
'law, that thou may'st not be examined
'at the last day.'

The King said, 'How am I to act 'according to law?' The flave anfwered, 'Grant me the liberty of putting the 'Viceroy to death, then order me to be 'punifhed, that thou may'ft kill me 'juftly.'

The King fmiled, and faid to the Viceroy, 'What confolation do you fee for 'yourfelf?' He replied, 'O mafter, for 'the love of thy father's memory fend 'this rafcal away, that he may not bring 'me into misfortune. It is my fault indeed that I did not obferve the inftructions of the wife men, who have faid, "When you quarrelled with a flinger, "you broke your own head by your folly: "when you aim your arrow at the face of "your enemy, take care that you yourfelf do not come within reach of his "fhot."

FABLE

FABLE X.

HARUN Alreſhyd, when the kingdom of Egypt was ſettled upon him, ſaid, 'In oppoſition to that rebel-
'lious fellow, who in the pride of the
' kingdom of Egypt exacted for him-
' ſelf the honours of God, I will beſtow
' the kingdom upon the very meaneſt of
' my ſlaves.'

They ſaid that he had a black, by name Heſib, who was ignorance in the extreme: upon this creature did he throw away the dominion of Egypt.

They tell a ſtory, that the underſtanding, conception, penetration, and capacity, of this ſlave, were ſo limited, that a multitude of the natives came to him complaining, and ſaying, ' We have juſt been
' ſowing cotton upon the banks of the

'river Nile: the rain came unseasonably,
'and the whole is destroyed.'

Hesib answered, 'Wool should have
'been sown instead of cotton, that it
'might not have perished.'

A wise man overheard this, smiled,
and said, 'If riches had been proportioned
'to knowledge, none would have been
'more unfortunate than fools; but Pro-
'vidence dispenses favours to fools, that
'the tribe of wise men may stare. Neither
'power nor wealth are the necessary
'effects of knowledge: nothing happens
'without the assistance of Heaven.—It
'frequently falls out, that the ignorant
'is happy, and the wise man miserable:
'the chymist died, tormenting himself
'with mortification; the ideot found a
'treasure under the ruins.'

FABLE

FABLE XI.

ONE of the ancient Kings had a mortal disorder, the subject of which it is improper to relate. The Egyptian doctors were unanimous, that there is no particular remedy for this disorder, except the gall of a man, which is peculiar for so many virtues. The King ordered them to send for it. They found a farmer's son, according to the description the doctors had given: they sent for the father and mother, and made them easy by bestowing great riches upon them; the judge pronounced, that it was lawful to shed the blood of a subject for the King's safety; and the executioner was preparing to behead the young man. The young man lifted up his head to heaven, and smiled. The King said, " In such a situ-
" ation as this, what can be the meaning
" of

"of your smiling?" The young man replied, 'The dependence of children should be on their parents; and they should seek justice from the King, and carry their complaint to the judge: but now the Father and the Mother, for the vanities of the world, surrender me up to be killed; the Judge pronounces sentence upon me, and the King approves it. I have no protection but in the Almighty; for to whom else can I carry my complaint from thee? Only then before thee, O King! do I supplicate justice from thy hand.' The King's heart relented at these words, and the water gushed from his eyes; and he said, 'Death is better to me, than to shed the blood of such an innocent person.' He kissed the head and eyes of the young man, held him fast to his bosom, loaded him with wealth, and gave him his liberty.

I heard that the King recovered that very day; and I had then framed an intention
of

of composing the following distich, that the keeper of the elephant should say upon the banks of the river Nile: 'O such a one! if you know the situation of a pismire under your feet, it is the same as your own situation under the feet of an elephant.'

FABLE

FABLE XII.

ONE of my companions came to me and complained of the world, saying, 'I have a small income, and a large
' family, and I cannot bear the burden of
' poverty: and it has often come into my
' head to go into another country; so that,
' let me live there as I please, nobody will
' concern himself about my good or bad
' fortune. Many people go to bed hun-
' gry; no one enquires, who are they?
' Many people die; not a soul mourns
' over them. But then, again, I think of
' the derision and scorn of my enemies,
' that they may insultingly laugh at me
' behind my back, and may explain my
' endeavours to serve my family as cruel,
' and a want of humanity; and may say,
" Don't give countenance to that worth-
" less fellow, for he shall never see the
" face of prosperity: he chuses ease for
" himself,

" himself, and leaves his wife and chil-
" dren to starve." Now of one thing
' I am certain, that through your assist-
' ance, an employment may be obtained
' for me at court, which may be the
' means of restoring peace to my mind. For
' the remainder of my life, I shall never
' be able to discharge my debt of gra-
' titude.'

I said to him, ' O brother, an employ-
' ment at court presents two prospects,
' the hope of subsistence, and the fear of
' life; and it is contrary to the opinion
' of wise men, to risk life for any expec-
' tation, be it ever so flattering.—Nobody
' comes into the house of a poor man,
" Give me the tax of your ground and
" garden." Either reconcile yourself to
' the torment of mortification, or expose
' your liver to be consumed by the
' crow.'*

He

* It is a custom with the Persians to produce their dead bodies, and let them lie in the sun. The meaning therefore of Sadi's allusion, in his advice

He replied, 'You have not said what
'is applicable to my situation, and you
'have not given an answer to my ques-
'tion.—Have you never heard, that who-
'soever cheats, his hands shake in reck-
'oning the money? Truth is the way
'to please God. I never saw any body
'lose himself by keeping the right road;
'and wise men have said, "There are four
"persons in fear of four persons; the
"highwayman, of the King—the thief, of
"the watchman—the villain, of the in-
"former—the drunkard, of the excise-
"man." But to him whose account is clear,
'what apprehension is there of being called
'upon? Be not prodigal in your office,
'if you wish that, when you relinquish,
'your enemy may have no power to hurt
'you. Be thou clear, O brother, and
'then

to his friend, is this 'Either reconcile yourself to
' the torment of mortification,' that is, ' Sit down
' easy under your disappointment, and trust not so
' precarious a dependence as a court.' ' Or expose
' your liver to be consumed by the crow,' that is,
' Expect soon to be brought into disgrace by your
' enemies, and perhaps sentenced to death.'

'then stand in awe of no one. The
'washerwomen beat only the dirty clothes
'upon the stones.'

I made answer, 'The story of the fox
'is similar to your situation.—They saw
'him running, and tumbling, and getting
'up again. Somebody said to him, "O
"fox, what is the matter that puts you
"in such a panic?" He replied, "I
"heard that they are taking a tiger in
"the net." The person returned, "You
"poor creature, what resemblance have
"you to a tiger? or what resemblance has
"the tiger to you?" "Hold your peace,
"says the fox, for if the enemy says on
"purpose, This is the tiger, and I am
"taken, who will give himself any trou-
"ble about my release?" Till the medi-
'cine for healing the bite of the serpent is
'brought from Erack, the person bit by
'the serpent may die. Apply the story of
'the fox to yourself: you have the supe-
'riority in knowledge, you have per-
'fections of every kind, moderation, and
'piety.

'piety: but your enemies are in ambush,
'and your adversaries lying in wait in
'a corner: let your disposition be ever
'so good, represent it otherwise and you
'fall into the King's displeasure. Who
'in that situation will have the power of
'speaking in your behalf? This conso-
'lation then is still left for you, to be con-
'tent as you are, and bid a farewel to
'greatness; for wise men have said, "In
"the middle of the sea there are treasures
"innumerable. if you want safety, it is
"on the shore."

My companion heard my discourse, was
enraged, turned away his face, and began
to say very bitter and disagreeable things.—
'What sort of sense is this? and where is
'the penetration, understanding, or know-
'ledge, in what you have uttered? This
'saying of the wise people is certainly
'true. Friends will be friends to you in
'a prison, but at the table enemies ap-
'pear friends. Don't look upon that
'man as your friend, who in your prospe-
'rity declaims upon friendship and good
'brotherhood:

'brotherhood: he is a friend indeed who
'takes his friend by the hand in the day
'of adversity and misfortune'

I perceived that he began to be uneasy, and interpreted what I said as uttered for my own purposes, and as if I was desirous of getting rid of him. I went therefore to the prime minister, on account of the old intimacy that subsisted between us: I told him the situation of my friend, and they appointed him to a small office. In a short time his abilities and capacity removed him from that, and he was established in a higher rank; and at the same time his prosperous fortunes increased so fast, that he arrived at the summit of his wishes, was near the King's person, and in great confidence. I rejoiced at his success, and said, * " Trouble

---

* 'To reconcile mankind to their present condition whatever it be, to teach them to bear misfortune with equanimity, in the expectation that better days may arrive, and to suppress a curiosity concerning future events, has been the object of all moralists —Sadi has

'not thyself in future with wishing, nei-
' ther be broken-hearted; for the water
' of the spring of life is in the dark: make
' not thyself unhappy at the revolution of
' times; for Patience, though it is bitter,
' bears a sweet fruit.'

About that time it was necessary for me to travel to Hjaz, with several of my companions. As we were returning home from our pilgrimage, he set out on a two-

---

inculcated this lesson under a wild and charming allusion, " that the water of the spring of life is in
" the dark;" and in a beautiful description personifies Patience, as the grand palliative of adversity.
" Patience, though it is bitter, bears a sweet fruit."
The Roman Poet, in a bolder strain, has expos'd the unprofitableness of this rash curiosity:

" Prudens futuri temporis exitum
" Caliginosa nocte premit Deus,
" Ridetque si mortalis ultra
" Fas trepidat."

But who can describe like Shakespear?
" O Heav'n! that one might read the Book of
" Fate,
" And see the revolution of the times
" Make mountains level, and the continent,
" Weary

two-days journey to meet me. I perceived inſtantly the ſudden reverſe of his fortune: he accoſted me—' Exactly as 'you obſerved, a party at court grew en-'vious of me, and charged me with 'theft——The King (may God preſerve 'him!) did not probe things to the bot-'tom: my old companions and intimates 'turned away their faces from the word 'of juſtice, and forgot former friendſhips.

" When

" Weary of ſolid firmneſs, melt itſelf
" Into the ſea and other times, to ſee
" The beachy girdle of the Ocean
" Too wide for Neptune's hips. how chances
" mock,
" And changes fill the Cup of Alteration
" With divers liquors! O, if this were ſeen,
" The happieſt youth, viewing his progreſs
" through,
" What perils paſt, what croſſes to enſue,
" Would ſhut the book, and ſit him down, and
" die"

Second Part of King Henry IV.

Never were lines penned ſo truly pathetical, and ſo uncommonly affecting, as theſe.

'When the world sees that Prosperity 'takes a man by the hand, they salute 'him with praises: as soon as they find 'his employment is taken from him, they 'trample him under foot. In short, I 'was encompassed with a variety of mis-'fortunes, till the day that the glad ti-'dings arrived of the travellers being 'returned safe from Hjaz; and then they 'released me from my imprisonment.' I said to him, ' At that time you paid 'no regard to the hint that I gave you, 'that the service of Kings is like tra-'velling at sea, profitable and danger-'ous: either you may gather the treasure, 'or you may die in the pursuit of it: 'either you may bring the prize safe to 'shore with both hands, or some day or 'other the wave may throw you dead 'on the shore.'

I did not irritate the wound of the poor man any further, nor did I sprinkle any more salt to enflame it; but concluded with these two distichs: 'You did not know
'then

'then that you was to see fetters upon
'your feet, when the advice people gave
'you did not enter your ears. Another
'time, if you cannot bear the pain of the
'sting, don't put your finger upon the hole
'of the scorpion.'

FABLE

FABLE XIII.

ONE of the Kings of Persia fell sick in his old age, and the hope of his life was cut off: on a sudden a horseman entered the door, and brought glad tidings of victory, saying, 'By the assistance 'of your Majesty's money and troops 'we have stormed such a castle, and 'have taken the enemy prisoners: the 'whole army, and all their adherents, 'have surrendered to your Majesty's 'mercy' The King fetched a deep sigh, and said, 'These glad tidings are not 'for me, but my enemies; that is, for 'those who shall succeed to my king-'dom. Alas! I have drawn on my be-'loved life, to this moment, in the expec-'tation that what my heart so earnestly 'wished for, I might obtain: I have

'now

'now succeeded in my most ardent de-
'sires; but what interest can I derive
'from them? for I have no hope that my
'past life shall return—the hand of Death
'beats his march upon the drum—O eyes!
'depart from this head—O knuckle and
'arm! every one of you, separate from
'each other—my time has passed in folly—
'—O mortals! I have done wickedly:
'but from my example beware.—The
'great enemy of all hath at last accom-
'plished his wishes in me—Help me, O
'help me, my friends!'

FABLE

FABLE XIV.

IT was asked of King Hurmuz, 'What 'crime did you see in your father's 'Viceroys, that made you imprison them?' He replied, 'No crime was proved 'against them; but I perceived that in 'their hearts their fear of me was exces- 'sive, and they placed no faith in my pro- 'mises. I was alarmed, lest, from the 'fear of their own lives, they might con- 'trive together for my destruction; there- 'fore I acted agreeably to the advice of 'the wise men, who say, "Be afraid of "him who fears thee, though thou art "able to conquer hundreds like him in "battle. Dost thou not know, that when "the cat becomes desperate, he plucks "out with his paw the eye of the leopard?

"So

"So the serpent stings in the foot his
"preserver, because he fears lest his be-
"nefactor some time or other may dash his
"brains out on the stones.*

* This fable affords a specimen of most detestable policy, worthy of Machiavel, and suited to the despotism of Asia.

FABLE

FABLE XV.

THEY tell a story of one of the Kings of Arabia, who stretched out the hand of Oppression upon the property of his subjects, and exercised violence. The people were forced, from his repeated tyrannies, to abandon the kingdom, and kept travelling on from the hand of his oppression. When his subjects diminished, and the strength of the nation was exhausted, and the treasury remained empty, the enemy's army attacked him. Whosoever wants a protector in the day of misfortune, say to him, 'Exercise generosity 'in the day of thy prosperity. If thou 'withholdest thy protection from the slave 'that is grateful, of necessity he must 'leave thee. Be not weary in acts of kind- 'ness, that thou may'st receive gratitude 'from the stranger.'

One day, in the King's presence, the people were reading the book of Shahnameh; and when they came to the story of the King of Zhak, and the days of Frydun, the Viceroy asked, 'Frydun had no 'resources either in money or men: how 'came it to pass that the kingdom was 'settled upon him?' The King answered, 'The people went over to him, and he 'gained it by their obstinate perseverance.' The Viceroy replied, 'The care and pre-'servation of the people is the very rea-'son why the sovereign is secure. Why 'then do you make your people desert 'you, except you have no desire of main-'taining your power? A tyrant can never 'take proper care of a kingdom; for it is 'impossible that a wolf can defend the 'flock. The King who commits acts of 'oppression, digs the wall of the founda-'tion of his own empire.' The King was offended at the Viceroy's reflections, turned away his face at these words, and sent the Viceroy to gaol.

A short

A short time after, the King's cousins rose up against him, and demanded a share of their father's kingdom. The people who had before been driven out by his tyrannies, joined them, and the right of possession was transferred to the cousins.

He who oppresses his subjects, makes his friends, in the day of adversity, his implacable enemies. Be at peace with thy subjects, and then thou mayest sit down fearless of the attack of the enemy; for to a just monarch his subjects are his defence.

FABLE

FABLE XVI.

I Saw a Constable's son at the door of the inn at Aghulmush, who had more sense, wit, perception, and knowledge, than can be expressed: even from his infancy the mark of greatness appeared on his forehead; and now his understanding being fully matured, it blazed forth upon his head like a star: in short, he was pleasing in the sight of the Sultan, because he united to beauty of features perfection of knowledge; and wise men have said, that dignities and reputation are the attendants upon knowledge, and are not bestowed by riches; and that true greatness is the companion of the understanding, and not the gift of old age.

His equals bore envy to him on this account, and contrived a plot for his deſtruction, which, if it had ſucceeded, would have been attended with no advantage. What can an enemy do if friends are kind? One day the King aſked him, 'What is the reaſon of their enmity to- 'wards you?' He replied, 'By the en- 'couragement of your Majeſty, I found 'favour with every body, but the envious 'perſon, whoſe only pleaſure is to ſee me 'loſe your protection. It is not in my in- 'clination to hinder any body; but what 'can I do with the envious man, who 'is his own tormentor? Die, oh envious 'man! that thou mayeſt be delivered out 'of this trouble; for a torment it is, 'and there is no deliverance from it but 'death.'

Bad people wiſh with ardent deſires deſtruction to the proſperity and fortunes of the good.* If the eye of the bat cannot ſee in the day time, what fault is there

in

* A moſt beautiful alluſion.

in the ray of the sun ? Speak truth. It is better that a thousand eyes should be blind like the bat, than that the sun should be dark.

FABLE XVII.

I Heard of a King who issued out his orders to put to death an innocent person. The innocent person, in a state of unhappiness, vented from his tongue abuse on the King; and expressed himself, as it is related, to this effect: 'He who is in-
' different about life, discloses every secret
' of his heart; in the time of necessity,
' when flight is out of our power, the
' hand grasps the hilt of the sharp sword.'

The King asked, 'What is he saying?' One of the Viceroys, a person of humane disposition, answered, 'He says, that he 'swallows his anger, is the forgiver of 'mankind.' Compassion touched the King in his favour, and he desisted from his intention of spilling his blood.

Another Viceroy, the very reverse of the former, said, 'It does not become us, who 'are subjects, to utter a single word, with-'out truth, in the King's presence. this 'person has abused the King, and said 'what is very impertinent.' At this the King turned away his face, and replied, 'To me that lye is more pleasing than 'this truth, which you have now spoken; 'for the one evidently tended to reconcile, 'and the other had its foundation in ma-'lice: and wise men have said, "A lye, "carrying along with it reconciliation, is "better than a truth conveying resentment."

Whatsoever a King says, that can he do. Wo to that King who speaks without a benevolent design! Upon the door of King Frydun's palace is written, in letters of gold, "O brother, the kingdom of this "world endureth not." Fix thy heart

on

on him who created it: place neither confidence, nor security, in this world; for many, such as thou art, hath it produced and destroyed. When the pure soul is ready for its departure, what is the difference between dying on a throne, or expiring in dust?

FABLE XVIII.

A Dervise was sitting alone in a corner of the desert: the King passed by him: the Dervise, having been made free of the city of Contentment, did not hold up his head, and paid no respect to the King. The King, feeling the pomp and splendor of royalty, was enraged, and said, 'This tribe of Dervises are like 'beasts.'

The Viceroy said, 'O Dervise! the 'King of the earth passed by thee—Why 'did'st not thou make salutation, and per-'form the ceremony of thy service?'

The Dervise replied, 'Say to the 'King, Expect service from him, who 'expects honours from thee. Kings 'are to watch for their subjects; not the 'subjects for Kings. The King is the 'protector

' protector of the poor, though riches are
' his for the support of majesty. The
' sheep are for the shepherd, but the shep-
' herd is to protect the sheep. One man
' thou mayest see happy to-day, and the
' heart of another pierced by misfortune.
' Wait but a few days, and the dust will
' consume the brain of the visionary. The
' thoughts of the King and slave are put an
' end to, when the written decrees of Pro-
' vidence are made known. When thou
' takest the dead body up from the dust,
' no one can distinguish the rich man from
' the poor.'

This saying of the Dervise made a strong impression upon the King: and he said, ' Ask me what favour you please.' The Dervise replied, ' One thing I request of
' thee, to give me no trouble.' The King said, ' Give me such instructions as may be
' of use to me.' He answered, ' Reflect,
' that riches are now in thine hand; but
' the riches of kingdoms pass from one to
' another.'

FABLE

FABLE XIX.

THEY asked Alexander of Macedon, 'In what manner did you subdue 'the nations of the east and west? because 'the ancient Kings had treasures and ar-'mies superior to thine, and yet such 'victories were not obtained.'

He replied, 'By the blessing of the 'great God, of all the kingdoms that I 'subdued, I did not oppress the sub-'jects of a single kingdom; and I never 'named the names of good men but with 'respect.'

Do not call him a good man, who mentions the name of the virtuous with contempt. Thrones, dominations, powers, absolute liberty of granting or refusing—

all

all these, when they are once past, are trifles. Do not destroy the good name of the dead, that your own good name may be kept in remembrance.

FABLE XX.

ONE of the Viceroys came before Zualnun of Egypt, and requested a favour, saying, 'Day and night I am em-
'ployed in the service of the King, ex-
'pecting a reward from his goodness, and
'fearing punishment from his anger.'

Zualnun wept, and said, That if Zualnun had worshiped God in the same manner, he would have been distinguished among the faithful. If there was no hope of rest and torment, the foot of the Dervise had touched the heaven. * If the Viceroy had feared God in the same manner he had feared the King, he would have been an angel.

* To this purpose our immortal Shakespear speaks, in the person of Wolsey
——————— " O Cromwell, Cromwell,
" Had I but serv'd my God with half the zeal
" I serv'd my King, he would not in mine age
" Have left me naked to mine enemies "

FABLE XXI.

ONE of the sons of Harun Alreshyd came to his father full of wrath, and exclaiming, 'The son of that vagabond 'there has abused me.' Harun said to his courtiers, 'What punishment is pro-
' per for such a person?' One of them gave his advice to kill him; another, to cut his tongue out; and another, to fine him. Harun said, ' Son, true generosity
' is, to forgive him; and if you cannot do
' that, go you in your turn and abuse
' him; but yet not so that the retaliation
' exceed its due bounds; and then the fault
' will be on your side. He is not a man,
' in the opinion of the wise, who seeks to
' fight with a strong elephant; he is a
' man indeed, who, when he is trans-
' ported with passion, does not utter a fal-
' sity.'

FABLE XXII.

THE Viceroys of Nushyruan were consulting together to regulate the kingdom; and every one, to the best of his capacity, struck out something. Abuzer Timoher approved of the King's idea. The doctors asked him privately, 'How 'came you to approve of the King's thought 'in preference of so many wise men?' He replied, 'Every one thought of some-'thing, and the thoughts of every one are 'in the disposal of God: nobody knows 'whether they will turn out right or 'wrong; therefore whatever is agreeable 'to the King's idea, is best: for if it 'should be the reverse of every thing that 'is right, by paying implicit obedience, I 'am safe from the King's anger; for it is
'said,

' faid, " To think differently from what
" the King thinks, is to wafh one's hand
" in one's own blood." If the King fays
' to the day, " It is night," we ought to
' fay, " There is the moon, and there are
" the ftars."

* If the doctrine of Paffive Obedience and Non-refiftance was not fufficiently underftood before, every difficulty is at once removed by this fable.

FABLE

FABLE XXIII.

ONE of the Viceroys was disgraced; he went and turned Dervise: the blessing of their company operated upon him, and his mind was at peace. Soon after, the King was reconciled to him, and offered him his place again. The Viceroy would not accept it, and said, 'O 'master! retirement is better than em-'ployment: those who sit in the corner of 'safety, shut the teeth of the dog, and the 'mouth of the people, the paper they 'tear to pieces, and the pen they destroy; 'and they are safe from the hand and 'tongue of the backbiters.'

The King said, ' I want a perfect wise ' man to be about me.' The Viceroy replied, ' O King, a perfect wise man is ' he who never exposes his person in such
' affairs.—

'affairs.—Thus the eagle preserves his re-
'putation, as king of birds, because he
'feeds upon dead carcases, and injures no
'living creature.'

FABLE XXIV.

THERE were two brothers: one was an attendant upon the King, and the other earned his bread by the strength of his arm. One day the rich brother said to the poor brother, 'Why don't you 'attend the King, that you may be re- 'leafed from the fatigue of labour?' He replied, 'Why don't you labour, that you 'may be released from the meanness of 'attendance? for wise men have said, "To eat one's own pittance, and to sit "down contented, is better than to gird "one's self with the girdle of gold in "slavery." To grasp hot iron in the 'hand, is better than to stand with the

'hand

'hand upon the breast, in the presence of a
'great man. Valuable life is wasted with
'thinking, What shall I eat in summer?
'and what shall I put on in winter? O
'impertinent belly! be satisfied with a
'loaf, that thou mayest not cause the back
'to be bent double in slavery.'

FABLE

FABLE XXV.

I Was sitting, retired from the world, by the grave of Yahya of Gylan. One of the Kings of Arabia, reputed to be an unjust man, came to me, made salutation, and desired a prayer for his success.—Poor and rich are equally servants at this door and this ground: but they who are very rich, are at the same time very poor.

The King said, 'Put up a prayer for 'me, as is the custom with Dervises, because 'I am in great fear of a fierce enemy.'

I replied, 'Shew mercy to the weak 'enemy, that thou mayest not be op-'pressed by the strong enemy. With the 'arm of power, and the strength of the 'hand, it is a crime to crush the poor and 'defenceless subject. He who is charitable 'to the necessitous, is under no apprehen-
'sion,

'sion, though his foot slip, that no-
'body will take him by the hand and
'assist him. He who sowed the seed of
'evil, with an eye to goodness, tortured
'his imagination for nothing, and made
'a false judgement of things.—Draw the
'cotton out from thine ear, and render
'justice unto the people: if thou dost
'not exercise justice there is a day of
'justice The children of Adam are all
'limbs of one another, and are all pro-
'duced from the same substance. When
'the world gives pain to one limb, the
'other limbs have no rest.—O thou who
'art indifferent to the sufferings of others,
'thou dost not deserve the name of a man.'

FABLE

FABLE XXVI.

ONE of the Kings of Khorasan saw Sultan Mahmed Sabactagyn in a dream, a hundred years after his death, when his whole body was decayed, and became dust: but his eyes were turning about in his eye-balls, and looking.

All the doctors were tired of thinking of an interpretation At last a Dervise explained it in this manner. 'His eyes have
' continued looking till now, because his
' kingdom is possessed by another. Many
' famous persons under ground are buried;
' a single mark of their having existed on
' the face of the earth remains not. That
' old corpse there, that they have deposited in
' the ground, the dust hath eaten to that
' degree, that a bone is not left. Still lives
' the

'the blessed name of Nushyruan, by the
'command of justice, although so many
'years have elapsed since Nushyruan died.'

Practise goodness, O mortal! and make some profit of life, before a voice shall pronounce, ' Such a one is no more.'

FABLE

FABLE XXVII.

A King was sitting in a boat with a female Persian slave: the slave had never seen a boat, and had never felt any distress: she began to scream and complain violently. The King's diversion was interrupted, and no remedy could be found to pacify her.

There was a wise man in the boat, who said, 'If your Majesty orders me, I can 'soon put an end to her noise.'

The King replied, 'It will be a great 'kindness and favour to me to do so.' He commanded them instantly to throw the slave into the river; and when she had had a few ducks, he took hold of the hair of her head, and brought her close to the boat. The slave, having seized the edge of the boat, came in, sat down in a corner, and composed herself.

The King was entertained, and said, 'What sort of doctrine is this?' The wise man answered, 'Before she had been 'ducked, she did not know the danger of 'drowning: In like manner he knows the 'value of safety, who has had an expe- 'rience of misfortune. O thou that hast 'appeased thy hunger! a loaf of barley 'seems below thy acceptance: my com- 'fort is what thou turnest from with dis- 'dain. To the angels of heaven, purga- 'tory is hell: ask the condemned wretches, 'they think purgatory a heaven. There 'is a great difference between him who 'presses his beloved to his bosom, and 'him who waits at the door, with the 'eyes of impatience, for his mistress.'

FABLE

FABLE XXVIII.

I Heard of a King who had spent his evening in jollity; and when he was drunk, he said, 'To me there is not a mo-
' ment of man's life pleasanter than this,
' because I am not plagued with thinking
' of the good or bad of others.'

A Dervise, naked from top to toe, had been sleeping without the door. He lifted up his head, and said, 'O King, there is
' none equal to thee in power—I grant
' that thou hast no sorrow—but what then?
' hast thou no concern about us?" The King pitied his situation, produced a thousand dynars, and said, 'Hold up your
' skirt.' The Dervise replied, 'Where
' should I find a skirt, when I have no
' coat?" The King's compassion increased,

and he ordered him a coat, with the money, and sent it him.

The Dervise devoured the whole sum in a few days, came again to the King, and said, 'Riches never stay with your men of 'spirit; there is neither patience in the 'heart of a lover, nor water in a sieve.'

When the King had no desire to see him, they brought in word that the Dervise was there. The King was enraged, and turned away his face. Wise men have said, "We ought to keep at a di-"stance from Majesty; for often their "thoughts are engrossed by important af-"fairs of state, and they cannot bear in-"terruption from the people."

Whosoever watches not a convenient opportunity, must expect nothing from the King's favour—'till you perceive the time when your words may have effect, don't expose yourself by talking away to no purpose.

The

The King said, 'Turn this miserable
'wretch out of doors, who in a few days
'has consumed so much money. The
'sums that are set apart for charity are
'the support of those poor who deserve
'charity, and not for such worthless fel-
'lows as this. The fool who burns a
'candle at noon-day, in the clear light of
'the sun, will have no oil left in his lamp
'at night.'

One of the learned Viceroys replied,
'O King, I think it expedient that some-
'thing should be settled upon these poor
'people, separately, for their daily sup-
'port, that they may not spend their time
'unprofitably: but the orders you have
'given, to turn them out, and to punish
'them, are repugnant to the principles
'of the truly generous. To encourage
'people, by first doing them acts of kind-
'ness, and afterwards to destroy their
'hopes, is unworthy of a wise man. A
'King cannot admit people into his pre-
'sence, and, when the door is open, then
'shut

'shut it upon them with violence. A bird
'goes where he may pick up something—
'he does not go where there is nothing.
'No one observes the thirsty travellers of
'Hjaz assembling upon the sea shore.
'Where there is a sweet spring, there bird,
'man, and insect, repair.

FABLE

FABLE XXIX.

IT is said, that Nushyruan the Just was roasting some game at a small hunting-seat, and there was no salt: he said, ' Take the salt at its price, and pay ' for it, that no wicked practices may be ' introduced, and the nation may not be ' impoverished.' The slave answered, ' What ruin can accrue to the nation by ' taking such a trifling quantity of salt ' for nothing?' The King said, ' The ' foundation of oppression was originally ' small in the world; but whosoever came ' into power has added something to this ' little, 'till at last it arrived to its pre- ' sent extent. But wise men have said, " If a King takes an apple from the gar- " den of a subject, his slaves have a right " to root up the tree: if a King seizes

" but

"but half an egg by force, his soldiers
" may spit a thousand birds."

FABLE XXX.

THE son of a holy man died: they asked what inscription they should put on his tombstone: he said, 'The verses 'of the Alcoran are too sacred to be writ-'ten in such places as these, because in a 'short time they may be rubbed out, and 'the people may trample upon them, and 'the hand of the clean and unclean may 'touch them: if they must of necessity 'write something, these verses are suffi-'cient. "Alas! when the green grew in "the garden, how my heart was delighted! "Friend, pass by in the season of spring, "and you shall see green growing out of "my earth."

FABLE XXXI.

I Never complained of the world, and never was grieved at the viciſſitudes of of life, except once, when I was not able to buy myſelf ſhoes.

I went bare-footed, and ſore at heart, into a moſque at Damaſcus. I ſaw a perſon there who had no legs: I immediately offered up my thankſgiving to the great God, and was patient at having no ſhoes.

FABLE XXXII.

ONE of the Kings of Persia (whom God preserve!) had a valuable stone in his possession, and had it set in a ring.—Once upon a time, he went out with his courtiers to walk in the valley of Shiraz, and gave his orders that the ring should be placed upon the top of a high dome, and whosoever should make an arrow pass through the ring, the ring should be his.

Very luckily there were then present four hundred experienced archers, who all missed the mark, except a boy, who happened to be shooting an arrow for his diversion—a favourable wind, by the interposition of Providence, conducted the arrow right, and made it pass through the

the ring.—The boy was recompenſed with garments and riches, and the ring was beſtowed upon him. The boy immediately burnt both arrow and bow. They aſked him, 'Why do you burn them?' He ſaid, 'That the firſt honour they have ob-
'tained me, may be remembered for ever.'

Sometimes it happens that the beſt concerted ſchemes of the fineſt underſtanding fail; ſometimes alſo, that an ignorant boy ſhoots his arrow at random, and hits the mark.

FABLE

FABLE XXXIII.

I Heard of a merchant who had a hundred and fifty camels loaded with goods, and forty slaves to attend him. One night, in the island of Kyſh, he took me into his chamber with his friends; for the whole night we had no reſt. He chattered his nonſenſe ſo plentifully: " Such a ſtock of mer-
" chandize is in Turkey—ſuch and ſuch
' goods are in India—here is the certificate
' of lands I purchaſed in ſuch a place, and
' ſuch a perſon is my ſecurity."—Then he ſaid, ' The weſtern ſea is very dangerous,
' and I muſt make one voyage more:
' when that is accompliſhed, I ſhall ſit
' ſnug in a corner for the reſt of my life, and
' content myſelf.' I replied, ' What voy-
' age do you propoſe taking?' He ſaid, ' I
' intend to carry the ſulphur of Perſia to
' China, as I have been told it bears a
' great

'great price there: from thence I shall
'take the China ware to Aleppo; the
'steel of Aleppo to Yemen; the slave-
'girls of Yemen to Persia; the silk of
'Rome to India; and the steel of India to
'Aleppo; then I shall leave off trade, and
'sit down quietly in my shop.'

In this ridiculous manner did he keep
prosing away, till he had not another word
left on the subject. 'But come, Sadi,
'(addressing himself to me) it is now your
'turn; recount to us something that you
'have seen or heard.' I replied, 'Did
'you ever hear, that in the desert of Ghur
'a traveller fell down from his beast, and
'said, " The greedy eyes of the covetous,
" either contentment must satisfy, or the
" grave?"

FABLE

FABLE XXXIV.

THE wife of a poor man was with child, and she never had borne a child in her life. she said, 'If the great 'God will bestow upon me a son, I will 'give all that I have in charity to the poor, 'except the gown on my back.' It so chanced that she brought forth a son: she immediately made rejoicing, and set out a table to treat her friends, as she had promised. Several years after, I returned from Sham on a pilgrimage. I passed by the place where the poor man lived, and asked how he went on? They told me, ' He had been a long time in gaol.' I enquired the reason. they replied, ' His 'son was overtaken in liquor, had a quar-'rel, and killed a man, and is fled out 'of the city. it is on this account that the
' neck

'neck of the father is in chains, and that
'his feet are in fetters'. I answered, 'The
'prayer of the parent has brought down
'this misfortune from heaven. O man
'of understanding! it is better, in the
'opinion of the wise, that women in la-
'bour should bring forth a serpent than
'wicked children.'

FABLE

FABLE XXXV.

IN the winter, a King with several of his courtiers went out to hunt, and found himself at a considerable distance from the palace: when night came on, he arrived at a small farm-house, and seeing the house of the farmer, the King said, 'Let us take up our abode there for this 'night, that we may not be exposed to 'the severity of the cold.' One of the Viceroys said, 'It is not consistent with 'the King's quality to petition a lodging 'in the hut of a mean villager: let us 'pitch our tent here, and kindle a fire.' The news reached the ears of the farmer: he prepared every thing that he had, carried it to the King, kissed the ground of salutation, and said, ' The King's greatness 'would not have been lowered by enter-'ing my hovel; but his courtiers did not 'care that an obscure farmer should be so
'honoured.'

' honoured' The King was taken with this obfervation, paffed the night at the houfe of the farmer, and the next morning beftowed upon him garments and riches I heard, that on the King's departure, the farmer run clofe by the stirrup of his faddle, and faid, ' The dignity
' of majefty has not fuffered by accepting
' the invitation of the villager; and the
' corner of the villager's cap has attained
' the fun's luftre, becaufe a monarch, con-
' defcending as thou art, has reflected light
' on his head.'

FABLE XXXVI.

TWO Noblemen were in Egypt: the one applied himself to learning, and the other accumulated wealth. In process of time the one had the reputation in Egypt of a learned man, and the other became King of Egypt. One day the rich brother said to the poor brother, 'I 'have obtained the kingdom, and thou 'still remainest in poverty.' He replied, 'Thanks be to God, holy and powerful, for 'this beyond every thing, that I have suc- 'ceeded to the inheritance of the Prophets, 'and thou to the inheritance of Pharaoh 'and Haman—that is, to the kingdom 'of Egypt. I am a reptile so insignificant, 'that the world may trample me under 'foot; not a wasp, that they may com- 'plain of my sting—How can I express,

'as

'as I ought, my gratitude for the riches of
'heaven's mercy, that I have no power of
'oppressing the people?'

FABLE XXXVII.

I Saw a Dervise, who was sitting in a cave, and had shut the door against the world, and looked down with the eye of pride upon Kings and great men. He who accustoms himself to begging, will be a beggar till he dies—Banish covetousness, and be the King of thy own pleasures—The neck of the generous man may be exalted with honour.

It chanced that one of the Kings of that country expressed a desire, that the Dervise should come and eat at his table, having formed great expectations from the disinterestedress and humanity of these

holy men. The Dervife, as it was a part of his religion to accept an invitation, confented. The next day the King went, defirous to know how he liked his entertainment: the Dervife rofe up, embraced the King, and returned him a thoufand thanks. When the King was gone, one of the difciples of the Dervife addreffed him, 'Your conduct this day towards the
' King, is contrary to your ufual practice:
' What is the meaning of it?' He faid,
' O fon, have you never heard this fay-
' ing?—The ear is very well able to go
' without hearing the found of the tabor,
' and the lute, and the flagellet: the eye
' may difpenfe with not beholding a garden:
' it is not effential to the head to have the
' fmell of the rofe, or the narciffus: if you
' have not a pillow ftuffed with feathers, you
' may repofe yourfelf on a ftone: if you
' have not a handfome bedfellow by your
' fide, you may fleep, reclining upon your
' own bofom: but this abfurd importunate
' belly cannot compound for trifles.'

FABLE

FABLE XXXVIII.

ONE year I was travelling with the people of Asham from Balluk; and the road was dangerous on account of the robbers. There was a young man in the caravan with us, of whom you might say, that from his strength he would play with a tiger; and he was also so formidable an archer, that it required ten men to string his bow: but he had been bred up in prosperity, and nursed in the shade: he had never seen the world, and had never travelled: the thundering sound of the martial drum had never penetrated his ear, neither had his eye seen the lightning of the brandished sword: he had never fallen into the hand of the enemy, nor had the rain of arrows poured round him.

I and this young man were accidentally running together: every wall that came in his way he pulled down; and every large tree that he saw, by the force of his arm he tore up by the roots. He was boasting away, 'Where is the tiger now, that he 'may see the fingers and palm of a stout 'man? and shew me the elephant, that he 'may have sight of the shoulder and arm 'of the brave!'

Just at this time two Indians appeared, and advanced towards us: in the hand of one was a stake; in the hand of the other, a stone. I said to him, 'What are you stand-'ing still for? Shew us *now* the strength 'and courage that you possess; for here 'is the enemy, who is come of course to his 'grave.' I saw the bow and arrow drop from the hand of the young man, and a trembling seize all his joints. Not every one who is able to hit a hair with an arrow that pierceth a coat of mail, can stand his ground in the day of attack of the brave people. We perceived no other remedy for ourselves, but to leave our accoutrements, surrender our arms, and escape with our lives.

When

When you have affairs of moment, send a man who has been tried, for he can take even the lion in the snare. A young man, though he has strength of arm, and is powerful as an elephant, will feel his joints in the battle quaking through fear. A man of experience is as well qualified to act in the field, as a wise man is to interpret the articles of the law.

FABLE XXXIX.

A Poor man paſſed by a rich man, who was binding his ſlave hand and foot, and puniſhing him ſeverely. He ſaid, 'O 'my child, he is a human creature like 'thee. God has made him ſubject to thee, 'and has given thee the ſuperiority over 'him. Why doſt not thou then offer up 'thankſgiving to heaven; and why doſt 'thou ſuffer thy ſlave to be thus tor-'mented and tortured? how doſt thou 'know but to-morrow he may be better 'than thou art, and that diſgrace may be 'thy portion? Be not tranſported with 'anger againſt thy ſlave; oppreſs him not, 'neither afflict his heart: thou haſt bought 'him for ten drams; but after all thou 'didſt not create him. How long will 'this inſolence, tyranny, and pride, laſt?
'One

'One Master there is, greater than thee.
'O thou that art lord here, with the
'lion's power, forget not thy own master;
'for the great Mahomet (the blessing of
'God be upon him, and salutation!) has
'left this sentence on record: "In the day
"of judgment it will be mortifying indeed,
"when the slave is received into heaven, and
"the tyrannical master ordered to hell."
'Upon the slave, whose services thou can'st
'command, exercise not an authority with-
'out bounds; neither be overtaken by
'passion for in the day of retribution
'how humiliating will it be, to see the
'slave set at liberty, and the master in
'chains!'

FABLE

FABLE XL.

A King was on the point of ending his life, and he had no successor: he made a will, that whosoever should enter the gate of the city first on the morrow, to him they should entrust the government of the kingdom, and place the royal crown on his head. Accidentally, the first person who entered the gate of the city, was a beggar, who had been accustomed all his life long to gather up fragments from the rich man's table, and darn the tattered pieces of his old garment. The courtiers and great men executed the will of the King, gave him the charge of affairs, put the government into his hands, and deposited with him the keys of the garrison and the treasury. The beggar had been King for some time,
when

when at last several of the courtiers revolted from their obedience, and the neighbouring Princes on all sides rose up against him: in short, his army was routed, and many cities were taken from him.

The beggar was sorrowful and dejected at what had happened, when one of his old friends, who had been his companion in his adversity, returned from a pilgrimage, saw him in this high situation, and said, 'Thanks be to God, holy and powerful, 'that thy good fortune advanced thee, and 'that prosperity has been favourable; that 'the rose is separated from the thorn, 'and that the thorn is extracted from thy 'foot. The bud for a time opens, then 'closes: the tree for a time is naked, then 'covered with leaves.' The beggar replied, 'O friend, what room is there for 'congratulation? When you saw me, a 'morsel of bread was my only concern; 'now I have the whole world for my 'care.' If we have not riches, we are uneasy: if we have riches, we make ourselves slaves, from the solicitude of preserving

serving them. There is no enemy fiercer than the pomp of this world; for whether you possess it or not, your mind is in torment: no rich man throws gold in your lap, till you have first flattered him for his charity. Often have I heard the wise men declare, "The contentment of "the Dervise is better than the charity "of the rich: if King Baharam sacrifices "an elk, it will not be more than the leg "of a locust to a pismire."

FABLE

FABLE XLL

ONE of the pilgrims of Sham was worshipping in the wilderness, and was eating the leaves of the trees—A King went that way, with an intention of seeing him, and said, 'If you think proper, you
' may come into the city, and a place shall
' be prepared for your habitation, that
' you may obtain a tranquillity of mind
' preferable to the misery which you now
' feel, and that others also may derive be-
' nefit from the blessing of your instruction,
' and may imitate the goodness of your ex-
' ample.' This saying of the King's was not agreeable to the pilgrim, and he turned away his face. One of the Viceroys replied, ' I
' advise you to come into the city, if it is
' only for a few days, out of respect to
' the King: if there should be any thing
' in the company of strangers repugnant
' to

'to the purity of holy perfons, you will be at liberty to depart.' They relate, that the pilgrim came into the city; they furnished for him a particular garden-houfe of the King's, and adorned this delightful place for his reception. The rofe of this garden was like the cheeks of the beautiful; and the hyacinth of it, like the locks of the beloved; and it was as pure and free from corruption, as a child that has not yet fucked the milk of the nurfe. The King immediately fent a handfome flave girl to wait on him, that at the fight of fuch a heavenly creature, the feducer of Abed, in brightnefs refembling the moon, and furpaffing the peacock in the elegance of her figure, the foul even of godly men fhould be rendered incapable of refiftance. After her, a male flave was fent, of wonderful beauty, and a fweet difpofition; as the poet has faid, "The eyes were no more fatisfied with beholding him, than the leper's thirft from the river Euphrates." Abed began to feed upon dainty morfels, to clothe himfelf

in

in costly attire, from exquisite sauces to acquire a relish for eating, and to gaze upon the beauty of his man-servant and maid-servant; as wise men have said, "The lock of the beloved makes prisoner of the sense, and is the net for the cunning bird: with all my knowledge I have lost both heart and reputation in pursuit of thee. Truly then I am the cunning bird; thou art the net." In short, his prosperity was his misfortune; for it has been likewise observed, "Whosoever is an instructor, a philosopher, a profound scholar, or a sublime poet, let him once descend to this low world, is like a fly in the honey." Some time after, the King had a desire to visit him: he saw Abed changed from his former appearance, with a fine white and red, sleek and grown fat, and reclining on a rich pillow, with a slave girl, as delicate as a fairy, standing behind him. The King rejoiced at his prosperous situation, discoursed upon different subjects, and at last concluded with saying, 'There are two 'sorts of people that I am a friend to—
'the

'the learned people, and the monks.' There was a very learned experienced Viceroy with the King, who replied, 'O master of 'the earth, it will be shewing your friend-'ship properly, to do good to both sets: 'to the learned people give money, that 'they may prosecute their studies; to 'the monks give nothing, that they 'may still remain monks. Whosoever 'is of a meek temper, and has a true 'affection for heaven, is a monk, with-'out the bread of charity, and the mor-'sel obtained by begging. The fin-'ger of the beautiful, and the ear of her 'who seduces the heart, are still beautiful, 'without the ear-ring, and the ring of 'sapphire. To the Dervise of humble 'soul, and a virtuous disposition, the 'bread of alms, and the morsel obtained 'by begging, are of no value; to a hand-'some woman, and a lovely face, paint, 'and ornaments, and the ring of sapphire, 'are of no consequence. As long as I 'possess one thing, and covet another, if 'people say, I am no monk, they say right.'

FABLE

FABLE XLII.

HEAR this tale.—In Bagdat a quarrel happened between the Flag and the Curtain. The Flag, incommoded by the dust of the road, and the fatigue of the stirrup, said to the Curtain, 'I and thou 'are both fellow servants; we are slaves of 'the King's court. I have no rest a single 'moment from service; and whether it is 'fair or foul, I must always be travelling. 'Thou hast never experienced hardship, 'neither in the fort, nor in the desert, nor 'from the flying of the dust. My foot is 'before thee in labour: What is the rea- 'son then that thou art before me in ho- 'nour? Thou art in the company of 'handsome slaves, and of maids whose 'breath is like the smell of the jessamine. 'I fall into the hands of soldiers, who are

'worn

'worn by travelling, and are always wan-
'dering about.'

The Curtain replied, 'I bend my head to
'the threshold, and not, like thee, lift it
'up to the sky. Whosoever exalts his
'head with pride will soon be thrown
'down from his height.'

FABLE

FABLE XLIII.

THEY tell a story of a boxer, whom misery brought almost to the brink of the grave. he went complaining to his father, and requested his permission to travel. 'Perhaps,' said he, 'by the strength 'of my arm I may succeed to my wishes; 'for wise men have said, "Learning and "ingenuity are of no service till they are "shewn: they put the wood of aloes be-"fore the fire, and rub the musk."

The father replied, 'Son, get vain ima-'ginations out of your head, and be con-'tented; for wise men have also said, "Riches are not to be obtained by bodily "strength; and the attempt to secure them "by mere dint of force, is as ineffectual "an experiment as to paint the eye-brows "of the blind."—If in every hair of your
'head

'kead there are a hundred accomplish-
' ments, accomplishments are of no use
' when fortune is unpropitious. What
' can a strong, but unfortunate man do?
' The arm of fortune therefore is better
' than the arm of strength.'

The son said, ' O father, the advantages
' of travelling are many: first, the satisfac-
' tion of mind, next profitable attainments,
' then to see wonders, and hear wonders,
' the view of cities, the conversation of
' mankind, the acquisition of honours and
' riches, the observation of friends, and
' the experience of the world.'

The father made answer, ' Son, the ad-
' vantages of travelling undoubtedly are
' many; but travelling is only proper for
' five sets of people.—The first is the mer-
' chant, who, possessing wealth and digni-
' ties, has slaves and slave girls, and active
' and laborious servants, to attend him:
' every day he may spend in a large city,
' every night he has a home to resort to,
' and every moment he may employ in vi-
' siting

' siting places of amusement and recreation,
' and gathering happiness from the gifts of
' heaven. A rich man is not a stranger,
' neither in the mountains, deserts, nor
' woods: wheresoever he goes, he pitches
' his tent, and takes up his quarters; and
' he who has not the good things of the
' world at his command, is unknown and
' obscure in his native country.—The se-
' cond is the learned man, who by uttering
' sweet sentences, and by the powers of elo-
' quence, and store of knowledge, in every
' country and clime finds people to serve
' and to honour him. The presence of a
' learned man is like pure gold, because
' whithersoever he goes, they know his
' sterling value and consequence. A poor
' nobleman stays in his own country; for
' in a strange nation they make no account
' of him.—The third is the beautiful, to
' whom even at first sight people lean, and
' incline with regard. It has been observed,
' that beauty is better than abundance of
' wealth; and they say, that a beautiful
' person is the balm of the heart, and the
' key of the locked door: therefore the

' world

' world thinks the company of such a one
' gain, and confers an obligation upon
' itself in obliging him. The beautiful
' person cannot go any where without
' meeting with respect and attention,
' even if the father and mother should
' turn him out with displeasure. I
' once saw the feather of a peacock in
' a holy book: I said, " This is an honour
" much greater than your situation de-
" serves." He replied, " Hold your
" peace; whosoever has beauty, where-
" soever he sets his foot, they pay him
" obedience." When in the child there
' is agreeableness and beauty, the resent-
' ment of the father is a trivial concern: he
' is a pearl, though the mother-o'-pearl be
' absent; and of a pure pearl every one
' will be the purchaser.—The fourth is an
' excellent singer, who, with his David-
' like throat, stops the water from flowing,
' and the bird from flying; then, by virtue
' of this accomplishment, he seduces the
' heart of the religious, and the learned
' dispose themselves for his company, and
' after

' after various manners oblige him. How
' sweet is a tender and soft sound to the
' ear! A charming voice is better than a
' beautiful face; for the one is the happi-
' ness of the wanton, the other the food of
' the soul.—The fifth is the poor and indi-
' gent mechanic, who gains a support by
' his labour, that his good name may not
' be disgraced for a bit of bread. If a wea-
' ver goes from his own nation in poverty,
' he suffers no distress, nor hardship; but
' if a king leaves his kingdom distressed, he
' sleeps hungry in mid-day.'

' The above-mentioned qualities, which
' I have explained, are a cause of comfort
' to the mind in travelling, and the pro-
' curers of solid pleasures: and he who is
' destitute of all these, may travel about,
' flattering himself to no purpose; for no
' one will either hear his name, or take any
' trouble about him. Whomsoever the re-
' volution of the heaven in malice afflicts,
' the world betrays. The pigeon, who is
' not to see his nest any more, fate con-
' ducts to the grain and net.'

The son said, 'Father, how am I able
'to contradict another sentence left upon
'record by the wise men? "Support is
"distributed to all, and to provide our-
"selves with those means, labour is necef-
"sary. Misfortune may be the decree of
"Providence; but it is our duty to pre-
"vent misfortune as much as we can. Sup-
"port may come of itself; but it is a proof
"of sense to follicit and toil for it by our
"own endeavours. Although no one can
"end his life without death, you have no
"occasion to run into the jaws of the dra-
"gon."— In my present situation I am
'able to fight with an elephant, and to
'contend with a lion; and I have, besides,
'this inducement to travel, that I have no
'longer power to bear the misery under
'which I now groan. When a man falls
'from his rank, and his dignity, what has
'he more to concern himself for? A
'rich man in the night-time can repair to
'an inn; but wheresoever the night over-
'takes the beggar, there is his inn. A
'good man is not a stranger, neither in
'the east, nor west; and whithersoever

'he

'he goes, there is the nation of his God.' He said this, took leave of his father, asked blessing, and departed: he had not travelled far, when he arrived at the bank of a river, where the stream was so rapid, that one stone was tumbled upon another, and the noise was heard at seven miles distance. It was so dreadful a water, that even the water-fowl could not rest there, and the smallest wave carried a mill-stone from the shore. He saw a multitude of people sitting down at the crossing-place, with money in their hands to pay the passage, and bundles prepared for their journey: the young man had no money, and threw himself upon their generosity; but the more he supplicated, the more he was disregarded. The inhuman boatman went away laughing, and said, 'You have no 'money, and you cannot cross the river by 'means of your strength—Of what avail 'is the strength of ten men?—Shew us the 'money of one.'

The young man was enraged at the insolence of the boatman, and wished to revenge

venge himself. The boat was gone off: he called out, 'If you will be satisfied with 'this garment which I have on my back, 'I care little about it, and I will give it 'you.' The boatman was greedy, and returned. Covetousness sews up the eyes of the cunning, and covetousness brings both bird and fish to the net.

As soon as the young man had fastened upon the collar and beard of the boatman, he dragged him towards him, and knocked him down without ceremony: his companion stepped out of the boat to assist him, and met with the same favour. in short, they perceived no other remedy for themselves, but to make peace with him; as wise men have said, "Where you see "fighting, be peaceable; for a peaceable "disposition puts a stop to contention: "where you observe quarrels, be calm; "for a sharp sword will not cut where "there is no resistance—with a sweet "tongue, and softness and gentleness, you "may move an elephant with a hair." After this they fell at his feet, and kissed his head
and

and face, then took him into the boat, and carried him over, till they came to a pillar that stood in the middle of the river: the boatman said, ' The boat is in danger;
' perhaps one of you, who is a strong and
' courageous man, will get upon the top
' of the pillar, and take hold of the rope
' of the boat, that we may disengage our-
' selves from the pillar.'—The young man, in the vanity of his strength, which he had boasted so much, did not suspect the boatman, and paid no attention to what experienced men have declared.—" If
" thou hast done an injury to another, and
" hast bestowed upon him a hundred kind-
" nesses afterwards, think not he will for-
" get to retaliate upon thee that single in-
" jury; for the arrow may be extracted
" from the wound, but the pain still
" rankles in the heart. Expect not to be
" free from affliction thyself, when with
" thy own hand thou hast afflicted the heart
" of another. Throw not a stone at the
" wall of a fort, for probably from the fort
" a stone may come levelled at thee."
What an excellent lesson Yektarch gave to
his

his friend! "When thou haft injured "another, take no comfort thyfelf."

As foon as he had gathered up the rope with his arm, and had reached the top of the pillar, the boatman cut the rope, and fet the boat adrift. The young man remained hopelefs and aftonifhed on the top of the pillar: for two days he fuffered feverely, and experienced a great deal of hardfhip: the third day fleep overtook him, and threw him into the river. After a day and a night, and after undergoing various fatigues and troubles, he reached fhore, and very fmall figns of life difcovered themfelves: he began to eat the leaves of the trees, and to dig the earth, till he recovered his ftrength a little, when he bent his courfe to the wildernefs, and arrived hungry, and thirfty, and faint, to a well. He faw a multitude of people, who were drinking a draught of water for a farthing: the young man had no farthing, and he befeeched them for water; but they had no compaffion upon him: he ftretched forth his hand

hand, and knocked several of them down: the men attacked him in turn, and beat him unmercifully, till he was sorely wounded. When the musketas assemble, they conquer an elephant, with all the strength and power that the elephant has. When the insects gather together, they strip the skin of the lion. In short, wounded and destitute, from necessity he followed the caravan.

In the night they came to a place reckoned dangerous on account of the robbers: he saw the people in the caravan trembling, and quaking, and looking as if they expected to die. He said, 'What 'is the matter with you?' They replied, 'This is the place for the robbers.' He answered, 'Fear not, I am here with you, 'and I can beat fifty men: the rest of you 'may help me, and give me assistance.' Their spirits revived at his boasting, and they rejoiced at having him with them, and they supplied him with victuals and drink.

The

The fire of the young man's appetite raged, and he had no command over himself; and he devoured so much in eating, and drank so freely, that at last the devil in him was laid, and sleep overtook him, and he slept soundly. An old experienced man, who had seen a great deal of the world, was in the caravan; who said, 'I am not so much in fear of the
' thieves as of your caravan: for they
' relate, that an Arabian once had col-
' lected some money; and all night, from
' the dread of losing this money, he had no
' rest: he requested the company of one of
' his friends, that by his presence the ap-
' prehensions he had, of being alone, might
' be removed: they say that his friend
' passed several nights in company with the
' Arabian, and when he had intelligence
' of his money, he robbed him, spent the
' money, and marched off The next morn-
' ing they saw the Arabian making dreadful
' mourning and lamentation: somebody
' said to him, ' What is the matter? per-
' haps the thief has taken away your mo-
' ney.' "No in troth," returned the Ara-
' bian,

'bian, "but the very man who should have defended it." 'I never sat without terrors from the serpent, when I knew what was his temper: the wound of the teeth of enmity is then worst, when it is given under the semblance of friendship. How do you know but this man may be one of the thieves, who by stratagem has introduced himself to us, that at a convenient opportunity he may convey information to his companions? My advice therefore is this, to reconcile ourselves to be robbed, if it is to be so, and leave this man asleep, and pack up our goods, and depart.' The advice of the old man was approved by the people of the caravan; and as they had a fear of the strong man in their hearts, they left him asleep, and departed.

The young man, when the sun shone on his shoulders, and ushered in the morning, came to his senses. he lifted up his head, and did not see the people of the caravan. he walked about backwards and forwards, quite out of heart, and desponding, and
could

could not find the caravan: he lay down with his face on the earth, and his heart almost broken, and said, 'They who have 'never experienced the hardships of travel, 'are the first to desert and distress the poor 'traveller.' He had just uttered this sentence, when, on a sudden, the King's son, being out a hunting, lost his attendants, happened to come to the spot where he was, overheard him, and looked at him: he remarked, that his outward appearance was favourable, and enquired about him. 'Whence are you, and how came you here?' He explained briefly to the King's son all that had happened. The King's son took compassion upon his distressed situation, bestowed upon him garments and riches, and ordered a trusty servant to accompany him, and see him safe into his own city. The father and mother rejoiced at the sight of him, and offered up a thanksgiving for his return.

That evening he enumerated to his father all his adventures: what had chanced

to

to him in the boat, the infolence of the boatman, the injuftice of the Turks at the well, and the pretence of the people of the caravan for leaving him.

The father faid, 'O fon, did not I tell you, when you fet out, that the 'hand of the ftrong, but poor man, 'is clofed, and his foot, though re-'fembling the paw of a tiger, broken? 'What an excellent faying is that of the 'poor wretch! "A grain of gold is better "than fifty pounds of ftrength."

The fon anfwered, 'O father, till you 'have borne fatigue, you cannot ob-'tain the treafure; and till you have 'endangered your life, you cannot con-'quer the enemy; and till you have 'fown the feed, you cannot reap the har-'veft. Don't you perceive, for the tri-'fling croffes I fuftained, what comfort 'I have brought back; and for the fting 'that I endured, what a ftock of honey 'I gathered? Although we cannot enjoy

'more

'more than Providence gives us, we ought
'not to be indolent about the means of
'acquiring it: the diver, if he thinks of
'the jaw of the shark, will never have a
'valuable pearl in his possession: the
'lowest stone of the mill does not move;
'therefore it bears a great load. What can
'a lion eat in his den? What mainte-
'nance can the idle procure for himself?
'If you sit still in your house, and want
'provision, your hand and foot will be as
'thin as a spider.'

The father said, 'O son, heaven has
'been merciful to thee now, and hath
'blessed thee with its assistance, till the
'rose has been extracted from the thorn,
'and the thorn has been taken out of
'thy foot, and a rich man met with thee,
'and was generous to thee: but such
'an event seldom happens, and wonders
'are not to be expected.'

FABLE

FABLE XLIV.

[This and the nine following Fables are upon *the Advantages of Education*.]

ONE of the Viceroys had a stupid son: he sent him to a wise man to be educated, till he should become sensible: the wise man instructed him for a long time, but his instructions were ineffectual. He sent him back to his father with this message: 'Your son will never be sensible, and he has very near turned my brain.' No polish will bring to perfection the steel that in its nature is bad. The jack-ass that carried Jesus into Jerusalem, if he was to go to Mecca, at his return would still be a jack-ass.

FABLE XLV.

A Wise man gave this lesson to his sons: 'My dear children, apply your-
'selves to knowledge, because we cannot
'trust the continuance of the kingdoms
'and riches of the world. Silver and gold
'are exposed to danger: either the thief
'may take them away at once, or the
'possessor may squander them by degrees:
'but knowledge is a living spring, and
'durable wealth. If a man of education
'loses his fortune, it is of little concern,
'because knowledge of itself is riches;
'and wheresoever the man of education
'goes, he meets with respect, and sits in
'the uppermost seat: but the man who has
'had no education, picks up scanty mor-
'sels, and experiences hardship; and how
'deplorable is it, after having been used
'to power, and pomp, and independence,
'to be insulted and despised by the peo-
'ple!'

FABLE XLVI.

TUMULTS and confusion happened in Sham: every one quitted his habitation, and left the city. The sons of a farmer, who were wise and intelligent, obtained the rank of Viceroys under the King: the sons of a Viceroy, who were illiterate and uneducated, were reduced to ask charity of the farmer. If thou desirest an inheritance from thy father, acquire thy father's knowledge: as for his riches, *them* thou may'st consume in ten days.

FABLE XLVII.

ONE of the learned men had a King's son to instruct: he beat him unmercifully, and reprimanded him without end. One day the boy, unable to bear his ill usage any longer, complained to his father, stripped himself, and shewed his body covered with bruises. The father was enraged, sent for the master, and said, 'You do not allow yourself to beat any
' one of my subjects in the cruel manner
' you have treated my son: what's the
' reason of this?' The master made answer, 'To discourse with judgment, and
' to have a pleasing, conciliating beha-
' viour, becomes mankind in general; but
' particularly Kings, because whatsoever
' they say, or do, is instantly published;
' and the speeches and actions of the rest
' of the world are not of such conse-
' quence. If a Dervise has a hundred
' faults,

' faults, of the hundred his friends cannot
' find one. if a King makes but one flip,
' it is circulated from kingdom to king-
' dom: therefore, in forming the minds
' of young princes, more labour and pains
' fhould be beſtowed, than on the vulgar.
' He who conducts himſelf ill in his in-
' fancy, in manhood will have no good
' qualities in him: when the wood is
' green, you may twiſt it which way you
' will; when it is dry, you cannot make it
' ſtrait, but with the fire.' The King was
charmed with the excellence of the maſter's
reply, and the manner in which he explained himſelf; beſtowed garments and
riches upon him, and exalted him to a
high ſtation.

FABLE XLVIII.

I Saw a schoolmaster in the west, who had a sour face, and a bitter tongue: his insolent behaviour offended the people; his conduct and disposition were so morose, that the very sight of him interrupted the pleasure of Mussulmen; and when he read the Alcoran, he disgusted his hearers. A multitude of beautiful boys and virgins felt the weight of his tyrannical hand, for he used to strike the silver cheeks of the one, and sometimes put the crystal legs of the other into the stocks. At last, being sufficiently acquainted with his character, they beat him, and turned him out, and gave his place to a pious, good man, of so meek and patient a temper, that he never spoke a word but when he was forced to it, and never said a single thing to offend any body.

body. The boys, in a very short time, had got the fear of their old schoolmaster out of their heads, and looked upon their new master in the light of an angel. Owing to his forbearance, they forgot all they had learnt: they were often found sitting and playing together, and breaking one another's heads with their uncleaned slates. When the master is good-natured, and relaxes his discipline, the boys clap their hands, and shout in the market-place. A few weeks after, I passed by such a church: I saw the old schoolmaster rejoicing, and happy, and restored to his former situation. I was vexed and said 'What! is this devil here? Do they 'appoint a devil a second time to in-'struct angels?" An old man, experienced in the world, smiled, and made answer, "Have you not heard what is related? "A King sent his son to school, and gave "him a silver slate under his arm: on the "top of the slate was written, in letters "of gold, *The severity of the master is* "*better than the indulgence of the father.*"

FABLE

FABLE XLIX.

I Saw a poor man, who succeeded to an immense fortune by the will of his uncle: he immediately plunged into every scene of riot and dissipation, and was elated with his prosperity: in short, he was guilty of drunkenness, and scarcely a crime can be named that he did not commit.

One day I talked to him: 'Child, For-
'tune is like a running water, and expence
'like a turning mill; that is, he may
'spend who has money to support his ex-
'pences: where there is no income, spend
'what you have slowly; for the song of
'the sailors is, " If the rain does not pour
" on the mountains, the river may be
" dried up in a year." Follow therefore
'my advice and instruction, and leave off
'these

'these idle follies and levities; because
'when your riches are gone, you may be
'reduced to hardship, and make a meal of
'sorrow.'

Accustomed to a gay life, and to eating and drinking luxuriously, he slighted my advice, and had no opinion of what I said. I perceived that he was deaf to my counsel, and that the warm breath of friendship had no effect on the cold steel of his heart. I bad adieu therefore to admonition, and left him; as wise men have said, "We point out the right "path to you; but if you will not take "it, the fault is in you."

Some time after, every thing that had before presented itself to my imagination, proved true. I saw him sewing pieces of his garment together, and scraping up morsel by morsel. I relented at his distressed condition, and thought, that in such a situation it would be inhuman to irritate the wound of the poor

poor man with the nail of reproof, and sprinkle salt to inflame it. I said therefore within myself, 'A weak man, in the 'height of his pleasures, does not look 'forward to the day of misfortune: the 'tree in summer produces fruit; in win-'ter, remains without leaves.'

FABLE

FABLE L.

A King sent his son to a Preceptor, and said, 'This is my son; educate him in the same manner as you would one of your own.' He replied, 'I shall obey your commands.' For several years after, he took uncommon pains with him, and did not succeed, when his own sons were completed in their learning and accomplishments. The King ordered the Preceptor to come before him, and said, 'You have broken your word with me, and have not performed what you undertook.' The Preceptor made answer, 'O King, education is the same, but capacities are different. Although silver and gold may be produced from a stone, in every stone there is not silver and gold. The star Canopus

'Canopus * shines all over the world, but
'the scented leather comes only from
'Yemen.'

* A star of the first magnitude in the southern hemisphere.

FABLE LI.

I Heard of an indulgent master, who spoke thus to his scholar, 'O son, if
'mankind had as much concern about
'God, as they have for their own support,
'they would be superior to the angels in
'rank. God did not forget thee, when
'thou wast an invisible drop, and un-
'formed: he gave thee a soul, understand-
'ing, capacity, and knowledge; beauty,
'goodness, discernment, thought, and reflec-
'tion: he furnished thy hands with ten
'fingers, and set two arms on thy shoulders.
'Dost thou think, O fool, that he will
'neglect to provide for thee?'

FABLE LII.

I Saw an Arabian, who said to his son, 'My child, they will ask you in the 'day of judgment, Bnaza aktſb vla ykat 'bmn abtt?' that is, *What have you done* '*in the world?*—Not, *Who is your father?*

FABLE LIII.

THEY relate in the books of the wiſe men, that the ſcorpion does not know its own birth, as the reſt of the creatures do; becauſe they devour the womb of their mother, and tear open her belly, and go to the deſert. I was once relating this myſtery to a wiſe man, who replied, " My heart bears evidence to the
" truth

" truth of this obfervation, and it will
" never be otherwife: for fince in their
" infancy they have dealt thus by their
" parents, they are defpicable, and hated
" in riper age." A father gave this advice to his fon, *" Young man, ftore up
" this leffon in thy memory—He who is
"ungrateful

* " Ingratitude ! thou marble-hearted fiend,
" More hideous, when thou fhew'ft thee in a child,
" Than the fea-monfter."
———" Filial ingratitude !
" Is it not, as this mouth fhould tear this hand
" For lifting food to't ?"

But in the following lines, to heighten the enormity of this crime, Shakefpear has exerted all the powers of language.

" Hear, Nature, hear : dear goddefs, hear a father !
" Sufpend thy purpofe, if thou didft intend
" To make this creature fruitful :
" Into her womb convey fterility,
" Dry up in her the organs of increafe,
" And from her derogate body never fpring
" A babe to honour her ! If fhe muft teem,
" Create her child of fpleen, that it may live,
" And be a thwart, difnatur'd torment to her :
" Let it ftamp wrinkles in her brow of youth,
" With candent tears fret channels in her cheeks ;
" Turn

" ungrateful to his parents, will never find
" a protector."

" Turn all her mother's pains and benefits
" To laughter and contempt; that she may feel
" How sharper than a serpent's tooth it is
" To have a thankless child."

I have heard these lines objected to, and indeed the whole play of King Lear, but particularly these lines, as *unnatural*. To such cold objectors, who are little acquainted with the peculiar province of poetry, Sir Philip Sidney shall give an answer.

" Whatsoever action, or faction, whatsoever
" counsel, policy, or war-stratagem, the Historian is
" bound to recite, that may the Poet, if he list,
" with his imitation, make his own, beautifying
" it both for farther teaching, and more delighting,
" as it please him, having all, from Dante's Heaven
" to his Hell, under the authority of his pen."

FABLE LIV.

[This and the Eight following Fables are on *the Advantages of Silence.*]

I Said to one of my friends, 'I am 'fond of silence on this account, be-'cause very often, in speaking, you may 'chance to say good or bad; and the 'eyes of enemies see nothing but what 'is bad.' He replied, 'It is better that 'an enemy should see nothing but what 'is bad; for in the eyes of enemies ac-'complishments appear faults Sadi is a 'rose; but in the eye of an enemy he 'is a thorn. The sun, illuminator of the 'world, the fountain of light, has no 'beauty to the eye of the mole.'

FABLE LV.

A Merchant loft a thoufand dynars: he faid to his fon, 'Take care that you do not mention a fyllable of this to any one; for I comfort myfelf upon your filence.'

The fon replied, 'Father, it is your command, and I will not betray you: ftill I wifh that you would explain to me, what ufe there is in keeping this matter fecret.'

The father made anfwer, 'That two misfortunes, inftead of one, may not befall me; firft, the lofs of my money; next, the reproach of my neighbours. Never difclofe your grief to your enemy; for enemies will only rejoice, and fay, *Labul!* that is, Poor inconfiderate fellow! it could not be otherwife—he had no prudence.'

FABLE LVI.

THERE was a young man who had made a great progress in learning, and had an uncommon quickness of capacity; but when he was in company with wise men, he kept his lips closed. One day his father said, 'Son, why don't
' you also communicate your knowledge?'
He replied, ' I am afraid, if they should
' ask me any thing, that I should not be
' able to give a proper answer, and by
' that means expose myself. You have
' heard, that a poor man was driving some
' nails into his shoe:—a stupid clown
' took hold of his sleeve, and said, " Come,
" shoe my beast." When you are silent,
' no one troubles himself about you; but
' when you *do* speak, speak sense.

FABLE LVII.

DOCTOR Jalinus saw an idiot, who had taken a wise man by the collar, and abused him: he said, 'Had this been 'a wise man, the affair with this idiot had 'not gone to these lengths: between two 'wise men there is neither animosity, nor 'ill-will; nor does a wise man contend 'with a fool. If a fool makes use of harsh 'words, a wise man wins his heart by 'forbearance. Two wise men will pre-'serve even a hair, when one obstinate 'and quarrelsome fellow will not: and if 'there are two ignorant persons together, 'they will break a chain. A malicious 'person once abused another: he endured 'it patiently, and replied, "*Sweet-spoken* "*gentleman*, I am worse than you can pos-"sibly represent me, because I know my "own imperfections, when you do not "know me."

FABLE LVIII.

THEY gave Saheban Vabel the reputation of being unrivalled for eloquence; becaufe, when he made an oration once a year before the people, he never ufed the fame word twice; and if by chance the fame word efcaped him, he explained it in a different manner: and of the many accomplifhments of courtiers this is one. Although a word be ever fo lovely and pleafing, and capable of receiving applaufe and confirmation, when you have uttered it once, do not repeat it, becaufe once tafting a fweet-meat is fufficient.

FABLE

FABLE LIX

I Heard of a wife man, who faid, " No one ever made fo true a confeffion of his ignorance, as he who, when another is fpeaking, and has not finifhed his fentence, begins talking. To every fentence, O wife man! there is a beginning and end—Do not thruft in a word between, to interrupt the difcourfe—The man of real difcernment, and penetration, never opens his mouth till he perceives filence."

FABLE LX.

SOME of the slaves of Sultan Mahmud asked Hussen Mymundy, "What 'did the Sultan say to you, just now, about 'such an affair?' He replied, 'It is no 'secret to you.' They said, 'You are the 'King's minister: how should the King 'disclose to such people as we are his 'conversation with you?' He replied, 'The King communicates in confidence 'with his servant, that he may be en- 'trusted with matters, and may not reveal 'them: therefore why do you ask?' A prudent man never publishes every thing that his sovereign says, because in publishing the King's secrets one ought not to sport with one's own life.

FABLE XLI.

ONE of the poets went before the chief of the robbers, and flattered him: the chief of the robbers gave orders to strip him and turn him out. The poor devil marched off, naked from top to toe, and the dogs fell upon him: he wanted to take up a stone, and beat off the dogs: the stones were frozen in the ground. He said in despair, 'What rascals these people 'are, to fasten the stones, and let loose the 'dogs!' The chief of the robbers looked out of a window, overheard him, smiled, and made answer, 'Here, master poet, 'ask of me a favour.' He replied, 'I 'want my clothes again: one may expect 'favour from good people; but, for my 'part, I have no expectation from thee; 'only don't injure me.' The chief of the robbers took compassion upon him, gave him his gown again, and, besides this, a garment of fur, and apologized for his pleasantry.

FABLE LXII.

THERE was a preacher with an unfortunate voice, who thought he had a most excellent one; he ranted away to no purpose, and his pitiable discourses had no effect. You would say, that his melody resembled the notes of the crow, and that the verse in the Alcoran, which describes a miserable voice, was intended for him. The people of the village bore with him, on account of the place he held, and did not think proper to hurt him. At length a preacher of that country, who owed him a grudge, went to him, and said, 'I have been dreaming of you' He replied, 'What did you dream?' The preacher answered, 'I dreamt that you had
'a charm-

' a charming voice, and that you lulled the
' people to sleep.' He recollected himself
a little, and said, ' This dream which you
' have had is a very good dream; for you
' have made me acquainted with my faults.
' I perceive that I have a bad voice, and
' that the people are tormented by my
' preaching: I promise another time to
' preach low. I am not satisfied in the
' company of friends, because they turn
' my faults into perfections, and make
' blemishes appear accomplishments, and
' shew my thorn for a flower of jessamine.
' Where then is the rude enemy without
' flattery, that he may set before me my
' imperfections?"

THE END.

Lightning Source UK Ltd.
Milton Keynes UK
UKHW05f0621150418
321065UK00005B/198/P